THE LAST FIVE YEARS

The Applause Libretto Library Series

The Last Five Years

The Complete Book and Lyrics of the Musical

Book, Music, and Lyrics by Jason Robert Brown

AN IMPRINT OF HAL LEONARD CORPORATION

Published in 2011 by Applause Theatre & Cinema Books
An Imprint of Hal Leonard Corporation
7777 West Bluemound Road
Milwaukee, WI 53213

Trade Book Division Editorial Offices
33 Plymouth St., Montclair, NJ 07042

Printed in the United States of America

Book design by Mark Lerner

Library of Congress Cataloging-in-Publication Data

Brown, Jason Robert.
[Last 5 years. Libretto]
The last five years : the complete book and lyrics of the musical / book, music and lyrics by Jason Robert Brown.
p. cm.
ISBN 978-1-55783-770-7
1. Musicals--Librettos. I. Title.
ML50.B878L37 2011
782.1'40268--dc22

2011007610

www.applausepub.com

PREFACE

I was walking to Lincoln Center Theater from my apartment on West 94th Street and I had no idea what I was going to say at the meeting. Thomas Cott had invited me to his office to talk about a commission for my next play, and he was expecting me to tell him about it. As I crossed 69th Street, an idea wandered gingerly into my mind, and luckily, I knew enough to grab on to it. By the time I walked three more blocks to Tom's office, I had sketched out the entire structure of *The Last Five Years*.

The less grandiose version is that I knew a couple of things before I started walking. Six months before, my musical *Parade* had opened at Lincoln Center Theater after four brutally hard (if thrilling) years of writing; and then it closed there less than three months later. I was determined that my next piece would be different from *Parade* in two important respects: first, I wanted it to be small in scale—two actors, so that it could be performed in any size theater, or even a concert hall or cabaret; and second, I wanted the songs to feel like, well, songs—one person having a complete musical moment, like a track on an album, without needing dialogue to tell the story. But who were these two people and what were they singing about? And if each song was essentially going to be a solo, then how did they interact?

The idea of writing a love story came simply enough; it seemed natural for a man and a woman to share the stage and tell the story of their relationship. But then I realized that if they were telling that story, then the relationship must be over. That explained why they weren't both singing at the same time. How to tell that story, though, without the piece becoming more and more relentlessly depressing as the evening went on? Wouldn't the whole second half of the show be nothing but morbid ballads?

That's when I hit 69th Street. What occurred to me was that She (whoever she was) had to start at the end of the relationship, and He (whoever he was) had to start at the beginning. And over the course of the evening, their timelines would completely cross, so that the show ended with him saying goodbye and her on the first date. That middle point, I realized, had to be their wedding, the one and only moment in the show when they would both be in the same moment onstage at the same time.

It's a peculiar truth that when I was coming up with all this on my walk, I wasn't thinking about my own life at all. Even though I was at that very moment embroiled in a terribly sad and bitter divorce, it didn't occur to me that the travails of this fictional couple I was choosing to create might end up overlapping substantially with the facts of my own first marriage. I even wrote the first song of the show without knowing specifically who these characters were— that song, "Goodbye Until Tomorrow/I Could Never Rescue You," is still in the show, more or less unchanged from what I wrote on June 15, 1999.

For the most part, I wrote the show from the outside in, always knowing that the wedding would be the last thing I wrote. (Turned out it wasn't.) In the course of bringing Jamie and Cathy to life, I felt myself exorcising the demons of my marriage, and certain clearly discernible facets of my and my ex-wife's personalities crept into these characters. It felt important to me to let those things be part of the writing—so much of the process of getting divorced seemed to be focused on blame and anger and money, and yet writing this show was about having faith that two people who loved each other could do the wrong things for the right reasons.

The Last Five Years changed my life in a great many ways. As a writer, the intensity and compactness of the form really forced me to strip my music and lyrics down to their essence—I feel like my work before *The Last Five Years* is occasionally gimmicky, "tricky," but I knew I couldn't get away with that on this show. In a way, it's my first grown-up piece. And personally, the process of experiencing the full arc of my marriage through a writer's eyes was considerably valuable in helping me heal, allowing me to close that chapter of my life with a sense of equanimity and move on to a wiser, more honest understanding of who I was and what I wanted a marriage and a family to be.

I'm grateful to discover that the show isn't really mine anymore. When the show is performed in Arkansas, in Mexico, in Korea, the audiences there aren't watching a thinly veiled version of me; they're watching Jamie and Cathy, and they're connecting to their struggle to love each other and find their own way as artists and people. Over the course of the decade, Jamie and Cathy have stood in for countless members of those audiences, and I hope they have given them the same comfort and closure that they gave me. I think they're good kids, you know. They made some mistakes, but they made them because they believed that loving each other was going to fix any problem that came along. It didn't, it doesn't. That doesn't mean they shouldn't have tried.

—Jason Robert Brown
Los Angeles, California
February 2011

THE LAST FIVE YEARS

The Last Five Years was first presented by Northlight Theatre (B. J. Jones, artistic director, Richard Friedman, executive director) at the North Shore Center for the Performing Arts, Skokie, Illinois, on May 23, 2001. Set and costumes by Beowulf Boritt, lighting by Christine Binder, sound by Rob Milburn and Ray Nardelli, casting by Mark Simon, musical direction by Thomas Murray, and direction by Daisy Prince. The cast was as follows:

JAMIE WELLERSTEIN **Norbert Leo Butz**

CATHERINE HIATT **Lauren Kennedy**

The stage manager was Patty Lyons.

The first New York production was presented by Marty Bell and Arielle Tepper, in association with Libby Adler Mages/Mari Glick and Rose/Land Productions, at the Minetta Lane Theater on February 11, 2002. The designers were the same as the Chicago production, except the sound designer, Duncan Edwards. The role of CATHERINE was played by **Sherie Rene Scott**.

SCENE 1
STILL HURTING

New York City at the end of the twentieth century. CATHERINE *is discovered. She wears a wedding ring. She is turning an object over and over in her hand—it is a man's wedding ring that matches hers. There is a note written on a yellow pad on the table—she has read it a number of times.*

CATHERINE

Jamie is over and Jamie is gone.
Jamie's decided it's time to move on.
Jamie has new dreams he's building upon,
And I'm still hurting.

Jamie arrived at the end of the line.
Jamie's convinced that the problems are mine.

Jamie is probably feeling just fine,
And I'm still hurting.

What about lies, Jamie?
What about things
That you swore to be true?
What about you, Jamie?
What about you?

Jamie is sure something wonderful died.
Jamie decides it's his right to decide.
Jamie's got secrets he doesn't confide,
And I'm still hurting.

Go and hide and run away!
Run away, run and find something better!
Go and ride the sun away!
Run away, like it's simple,
Like it's right . . .

JAMIE *enters—he's not wearing a wedding ring.* CATHERINE *does not see him. It is five years earlier than the scene in* CATHERINE*'s room—* JAMIE *is at the beginning of the relationship, and* CATHERINE, *across the stage, is at the end.*

Give me a day, Jamie!
Bring back the lies,

Hang them back on the wall!
Maybe I'd see
How you could be
So certain that we
Had no chance at all.

Jamie is over and where can I turn?
Covered with scars I did nothing to earn?
Maybe there's somewhere a lesson to learn,
But that wouldn't change the fact,
That wouldn't speed the time,
Once the foundation's cracked
And I'm
Still hurting.

The lights fade out on her and become stronger on JAMIE *across the stage.*

SCENE 2
SHIKSA GODDESS

JAMIE is saying goodbye to CATHERINE at the end of their first date.

JAMIE

I'm breaking my mother's heart.
The longer I stand looking at you,
The more I hear it splinter and crack
From ninety miles away.

I'm breaking my mother's heart.
The JCC of Spring Valley is shaking
And crumbling to the ground,
And my grandfather's rolling,
Rolling in his grave.

If you had a tattoo, that wouldn't matter.
If you had a shaved head, that would be cool.
If you came from Spain or Japan
Or the back of a van—
Just as long as you're not from Hebrew school—
I'd say, "Now I'm getting somewhere!

I'm finally breaking through!"
I'd say, "Hey! Hey! Shiksa goddess!
I've been waiting for someone like you."

A couple of days later.
JAMIE *is on the phone*
with CATHERINE.

I've been waiting through Danica Schwartz and Erica Weiss
And the Handelman twins.
I've been waiting through Heather Greenblatt, Annie Mincus,
Karen Pincus, and Lisa Katz.
And Stacy Rosen, Ellen Kaplan, Julie Silber, and Janie Stein.
I've had Shabbas dinners on Friday nights
With every Shapiro in Washington Heights,
But the minute I first met you
I could barely catch my breath.
I've been standing for days with the phone in my hand,
Like an idiot, scared to death.
I've been wand'ring through the desert!
I've been beaten, I've been hit!
My people have suffered for thousands of years
And I don't give a shit!

If you had a pierced tongue, that wouldn't matter.
If you once were in jail or you once were a man,
If your mother and your brother had "relations" with each other
And your father was connected to the Gotti clan,
I'd say, "Well, nobody's perfect!"
It's tragic but it's true.
I'd say, "Hey! Hey! Shiksa goddess!
I've been waiting for someone like . . ."

He hangs up the phone—maybe they are walking together through the park.

You, breaking the circle,
You, taking the light.
You, you are the story I should write—
I have to write!

If you drove an R.V., that wouldn't matter!
If you like to drink blood, I think it's cute.
If you've got a powerful connection to your firearm collection,
I say, Draw a bead and shoot!
I'm your Hebrew slave, at your service!
Just tell me what to do!
I say, Hey, hey, hey, hey!
I've been waiting for someone,
I've been praying for someone,
I think that I could be in love with someone
Like you!

Blackout.

SCENE 3
SEE I'M SMILING

Three months before Scene 1. CATHERINE *is sitting at the end of a pier by the river in Ohio—*JAMIE *has come, somewhat unexpectedly, for a visit. Over her dress she wears a sweater that's a little too small and not the right color.*

CATHERINE

I guess I can't believe you really came
And that we're sitting on this pier.
See, I'm smiling—
That means I'm happy that you're here.

I stole this sweater from the costume shop—
It makes me look like Daisy Mae.
See, we're laughing—
I think we're gonna be okay.

I mean, we'll have to try a little harder
And bend things to and fro
To make this love as special
As it was five years ago.
I mean, you made it to Ohio!
Who knows where else we can go?

I think you're really gonna like this show.
I'm pretty sure it doesn't suck.
See, you're laughing, and I'm smiling,
By a river in Ohio
And you're mine . . .
We're doing fine.

Five years earlier, just after their first date— Lights up on JAMIE, *on the phone in his studio apartment, a little nervous, calling a literary agent.*

JAMIE Hi, I'm calling for Ms. Whitfield. Yeah, my name is Jamie Wellerstein, and my professor at Columbia said he had called and . . . Yeah, Dr. Adler. Right. Oh, yeah, I mean, it's just a draft, but I think it's, you know, getting to . . . whatever. Well, look, I don't know from agents, Dr. Adler just suggested . . . Okay. Should I drop it off in person or . . . Um, yeah, I'll drop it in the mail then, that's great. No, that's great, thank you. What's your address?

Lights down on JAMIE.

CATHERINE

I think we both can see what could be better—
I'll own when I was wrong.
With all we've had to go through,
We'll end up twice as strong.
And so we'll start again this weekend,
And just keep rolling along . . .

*Her face falls—*JAMIE *has just told her he'll be leaving tomorrow.*

I didn't know you had to go so soon.
I thought we had a little time . . .
Look, whatever, if you have to,
Then you have to, so whatever.
It's all right—
We'll have tonight.

Back to JAMIE, *a couple of weeks later. Lights up as he picks up the phone.*

JAMIE Hello? This is. Oh, Ms. Whitfield, it's a pleasure to hear from you. And a surprise. Oh, you read it. Great, that's . . . Thank you so much, that means a lot to me. Yes, I really am twenty-three. Sure, whenever is convenient. Tuesday, good, nine o'clock, I'm there. I'm really looking forward to meeting you, Ms. Whitfield. Okay, Linda, thank you. Thank you, this is great.

Lights down as he hangs up.

CATHERINE
You know what makes me crazy?
I'm sorry, can I say this?
You know what makes me nuts?
The fact that we could be together,
Here together,
Sharing our night, spending our time,
And you are gonna choose someone else to be with—no, you *are*.
Yes, Jamie, that's exactly what you're doing:
You could be here with me,
Or be there with them—
As usual, guess which you pick!

No, Jamie, you do not *have* to go to another party
With the same twenty jerks you already know.
You could stay with your wife on her fucking birthday
And you could, God forbid, even see my show.
And I know in your soul it must drive you crazy
That you won't get to play with your little girlfriends—
No I'm not, no I'm *not*!—and the point is, Jamie,
That you can't spend a single day
That's not about

You and you and nothing but you.
"Mahvelous" novelist, you!
Isn't he wonderful, just twenty-eight!
The savior of writing!
You and you and nothing but you—
Miles and piles of you,
Pushing through windows and bursting through walls

En route to the sky!
And I . . .

I swear to God I'll never understand
How you can stand there, straight and tall,
And see I'm crying,
And not do anything at all . . .

The lights start to rise on JAMIE*'s side. He looks perplexed but not unhappy, as he dials. The lights stay up on* CATHERINE *for a bit, while she continues to cry, then fade during* JAMIE*'s call.*

JAMIE Rob? Yeah, listen. You know how my lease is up? You know how I want to get a new apartment? What if I said I was gonna get one with Cathy? Rob? Yeah, I'll meet you there in five minutes.

SCENE 4
MOVING TOO FAST

JAMIE

Did I just hear an alarm start ringing?
Did I see sirens go flying past?
Though I don't know what tomorrow's bringing,
I've got a singular impression things are moving too fast.

I'm gliding smooth as a figure skater,
I'm riding hot as a rocket blast—
I just expected it ten years later.
I've got a singular impression things are moving too fast.

And you say, "Oh, no,
Step on the brakes,
Do whatever it takes,
But stop this train!
Slow, slow! The light's turning red!"
But I say, "No! No!
Whatever I do,
I barrel on through,
And I don't complain.
No matter what I try, I'm flyin' full speed ahead!"

I'm never worried to walk the wire.
I won't do anything just half-assed,
But with the stakes getting somewhat higher,
I've got a singular impression things are moving too fast.

I found a woman I love,
And I found an agent who loves me—
Things might get bumpy, but

Some people analyze ev'ry detail,
Some people stall when they can't see the trail,
Some people freeze out of fear that they'll fail,
But I keep rollin' on.

Some people can't get success with their art,
Some people never feel love in their heart,
Some people can't tell the two things apart,
But I keep rollin' on.

Oh, oh—maybe I can't follow through,
But oh, oh—what else am I s'pposed to do?

The lights come up on CATHERINE, *making a call. Throughout the call, she is very consciously using her "professional" voice.*

CATHERINE Hello, this is Catherine Hiatt, I'm calling for Mike Stelmyer—thank you. [*She's on hold.*] Hi, Mike, it's Cathy

Hiatt—no, this won't be long, I'm sorry if I'm interrupting. Well, two things—I was checking to make sure you got the reviews I sent from this summer—yes, I got some nice notices from the local papers. I thought you would enjoy them. Okay, well, I can send out another set of those, sure. Right, well, the other thing was just, you know, checking in, seeing if you saw anything you wanted to send me in for, I feel like I'm in a really good place right now . . . Yes. Yes, I certainly will, as soon as I'm doing something in the city, I will make sure I let you know . . . Oh, okay, I understand. Thanks for taking the time, Mike—I'll call you soon!

She holds the phone for a minute, trying not to feel rejected, then puts it on its cradle. Lights down on CATHERINE.

JAMIE

I dreamed of writing like the high and mighty—
Now I'm the subject of a bidding war!
I met my personal Aphrodite—
I'm doing things I never dreamed of before!

We start to take the next step together—
Found an apartment on Seventy-third!
The Atlantic Monthly's printing my first chapter—
Two thousand bucks without rewriting one word!

I left Columbia and don't regret it—
I wrote a book and Sonny Mehta read it!
My heart's been stolen!

My ego's swollen!
I just keep rollin' along!

And I think, "Well, well, what else is in store?
Got all this and more
Before twenty-four!"
It's hard not to be sure I'm spinning out of control!
Out of control!

I'm feeling panicked and rushed and hurried!
I'm feeling outmaneuvered and outclassed,
But I'm so happy I can't get worried
About this singular impression—
I've got a singular impression things are moving too fast!

Blackout.

SCENE 5
A PART OF THAT

Eight months before Scene 3. A book-signing party for JAMIE*'s just-released novel.* CATHERINE *is sitting idly next to a pile of* JAMIE*'s books while* JAMIE *signs them. Someone has asked her what it's like being married to* JAMIE.

CATHERINE

One day we're just like
Leave It to Beaver.
One day it's just a
Typical life,
And then he's off on
A trip to Jamie-land:
Staring catatonic out the window,
Barely even breathing all the while . . .

And then he'll smile,
His eyes light up, and deep within the ground,

Without a sound,
A moment comes to life,
And I'm a part of that.
I'm a part of that.
I'm a part of that.

Next day it's just like
It never happened—
We're making dinners,
We're making plans.
Then he gets on the
Mule train to Jamie-land:
Handful after handful of Doritos,
Circling the apartment, logging miles . . .

And then he smiles,
His eyes light up, and how can I complain?
Yes, he's insane,
But look what he can do,
And I'm a part of that.
I'm a part of that.
I'm a part of that . . .

And it's true,
I tend to follow in his stride,
Instead of side by side,
I take his cue.
True, but there's no question, there's no doubt—
I said I'd stick it out
And follow through,
And when I do—

Then he smiles,
And where else can I go?
I didn't know
The rules do not apply.
And then he smiles,
And nothing else makes sense
While he invents
The world that's passing by,
And I'm a part of that.
I'm a part of that.
I'm a part of that,
Aren't I?

I'm a part of that,
I'm a part of that.
I'm a part of that.

At some point, she picked up a book—now she starts to give the book back, looks briefly at the dedication page, then quickly closes the book and hands it over.

SCENE 6
THE SCHMUEL SONG

Their second Christmas together. JAMIE *hits a switch and the lights on the Christmas tree are illuminated.* JAMIE *has a small gift-wrapped box in his hand. He holds it out toward* CATHERINE, *then mischievously takes it back.*

JAMIE Ah! First, a story. New and unpublished. A little Christmas story. I call it "The Story of Schmuel, Tailor of Klimovich." Merry Christmas.

He pulls a pad out of his back pocket—it is absolutely covered with scribbles and would be completely indecipherable to anyone but JAMIE *himself. He clears his*

throat melodramatically
and begins to read.

Schmuel would work 'til half-past ten at his tailor shop in Klimovich,
Get up at dawn and start again with the hems and pins and twist.
Forty-one years had come and gone at his tailor shop in Klimovich.
Watching the winters soldier on, there was one thing Schmuel missed.

"If I only had time," old Schmuel said,
"I would build the dress that's in my head,
A dress to fire
The mad desire
Of girls from here to Minsk,
But I have no more hours left to sew."
Then the clock upon the wall began to glow . . .

And the clock said:
"Na na na na, na na na,
Oh, Schmuel, you'll get to be happy!
Na na na na, na na na,
I give you unlimited time!
Na na na na, na na na,
So, Schmuel, go sew and be happy!"
But Schmuel said, "No, no, it's not my lot—
I've gotta make do with the time I've got."

Schmuel was done at half-past ten and he said, "Good night, old Klimovich,"

Put on his coat to go, but then the clock cried, "Wait! Not yet!
Even though you're not wise or rich, you're the finest man in Klimovich!
Listen up, Schmuel—make one stitch and you'll see what you can get!"

But Schmuel said, "Clock, it's much too late.
I'm at peace with life, I accept my fate . . ."
But the clock said, "Schmuel!
One stitch and you will
Unlock the dreams you've lost!"

So Schmuel, with reluctance, took his thread.
He pulled a bolt of velvet and he said:
"I should take out my teeth and go to bed,
I'm sitting here with talking clocks instead!"

And the clock said:
"Na na na na, na na na,
Oh, Schmuel, you'll get to be happy!
Na na na na, na na na,
I give you unlimited time!
Na na na na, na na na,
Just do it and you can be happy!"

So Schmuel put the thread through the needle's eye
And the moon stared down from a starless sky,
And he pushed the thread through the velvet black
And he looked, and the clock was turning . . . back!

So he grabbed his shears and he cut some lace
As the hands reversed on the old clock's face!

And his fingers flew and the fabric swirled—
It was nine-fifteen all around the world!

Ev'ry cut and stitch was a perfect fit,
As if God Himself were controlling it!
And Schmuel cried, through a rush of tears,
"Take me back! Take me back all forty-one years!"

And on it went, down that silent street,
'Til Schmuel's dress was at last complete,
And he stretched his arms, and he closed his eyes,
And the morning sun finally started to rise.

And the dress he made on that endless night
Was a dress that would make any soul take flight!
Not a swatch, not a skein had gone to waste—
Ev'ry ribbon and button ideally placed,
And sewn into the seams
Were forty-one seasons of dreams
Dreams that you could feel
Coming real.

And that very dress, so the papers swore,
Was the dress a girl in Odessa wore
On the day she promised forevermore
To love a young man named Schmuel
Who only one day before
Had knocked at her kitchen door.

Finished with the story,
he puts the pad back in

his pocket and takes out the little box again.

Plenty have hoped and dreamed and prayed, but they can't get out of Klimovich.
If Schmuel had been a cute *goyishe* maid, he'd've looked a lot like you.
Maybe it's just that you're afraid to go out onto a limb-ovich.
Maybe your heart's completely swayed, but your head can't follow through.

But shouldn't I want the world to see
The brilliant girl who inspires me?
Don't you think that now's a good time to be
The ambitious freak you are?
Say goodbye to wiping ashtrays at the bar!
Say hello to Cathy Hiatt, big-time star!
'Cause I say:
Na na na na, na na na na
Cathy, you get to be happy!
Na na na na, na na na
I give you unlimited time!
Na na na na, na na na
Stop temping and go and be happy!

He pulls a magazine and a business card from his back pocket.

Here's a headshot guy and a new *BackStage,*
Where you're right for something on ev'ry page—

Take a breath,
Take a step,
Take a chance . . .

And now he opens the top half of the little box and takes out a lovely watch.

Take your time.

Have I mentioned today
How lucky I am
To be in love with you?

The lights fade.

SCENE 7
A SUMMER IN OHIO

Six months before Scene 5.
CATHERINE, *writing a letter to* JAMIE.

CATHERINE

I could have a mansion on a hill.
I could lease a villa in Seville,
But it wouldn't be as nice
As a summer in Ohio
With a gay midget named Karl
Playing Tevye and Porgy.

I could wander Paris after dark,
Take a carriage ride through Central Park,
But it wouldn't be as nice
As a summer in Ohio,
Where I'm sharing a room
With a "former" stripper and her snake:
Wayne.

I could have a satchel full of dollar bills,
Cures for all the nation's ills,

Pills to make a lion purr;
I could be in line to be the British Queen,
Look like I was seventeen,
Still I'm certain I'd prefer
To be going slowly batty
Forty miles east of Cincinnati.

I could shove an ice pick in my eye,
I could eat some fish from last July,
But it wouldn't be as awful
As a summer in Ohio
Without cable, hot water,
Vietnamese food,
Or you.

I saw your book at a Borders in Kentucky
Under a sign that said "New and Recommended."
I stole a look at your picture on the inside sleeve,
And then I couldn't leave.

Richard, who was with me, got uncharacteristically quiet,
Then he said, "All things considered, I guess you don't have to buy it."
So I smiled like Mona Lisa and I lay my Visa down!
He wants me, he wants me,
But he ain't gonna get me!
I've found my guiding light—
I tell the stars each night:
"Look at me! Look at him! Son of a bitch!
I guess I'm doing something right!
I finally got something right!"

No, it's not Nirvana, but it's on the way.
I play Anita at the matinee,
Then I'll get on my knees and pray
I can state in my next bio:
I'm never gonna go back to Ohio!

I could chew on tin foil for a spell!
I could get a root canal in Hell,
But it wouldn't be as swell
As this summer is gonna be!
'Cause the torture is just exquisite
While I'm waiting for you to visit,
So hurry up, schmuck, get unstuck and get on the scene!
Love,
The Midget, the Stripper, Wayne the Snake
And Mrs. Jamie Wellerstein—
That's me!

Blackout.

SCENE 8
THE NEXT TEN MINUTES

JAMIE on a boat on the lake in Central Park, pointing to the apartment buildings on the Upper West Side.

JAMIE

No, that one's Jerry Seinfeld.
That one's John Lennon there.
No, the Dakota—
The San Remo is up a few blocks.
Have you been inside the Museum?
We should go.
Meet the dinosaurs.

Cathy.

He takes a ring out of his jeans pocket.

Will you share your life with me
For the next ten minutes?

For the next ten minutes:
We can handle that.
We could watch the waves,
We could watch the sky,
Or just sit and wait
As the time ticks by,
And if we make it 'til then,
Can I ask you again
For another ten?

CATHERINE *appears, wearing her wedding gown, and walks slowly toward the boat.*

And if you in turn agree
To the next ten minutes,
And the next ten minutes,
'Til the morning comes,
Then just holding you
Might compel me to
Ask you for more.
There are so many lives I want to share with you—
I will never be complete until I do.

JAMIE *slides the ring on* CATHERINE*'s finger.*

CATHERINE

I am not always on time.
Please don't expect that from me.
I will be late,

But if you can just wait,
I will make it eventually.

Not like it's in my control,
Not like I'm proud of the fact,
But anything other than being exact-
Ly on time, I can do.

I don't know why people run.
I don't know why things fall through.
I don't know how anybody survives in this life
Without someone like you.
I could protect and preserve,
I could say no and goodbye,
But why, Jamie, why?

I want to be your wife.
I want to bear your child.
I want to die
Knowing I
Had a long, full life in your arms.
That I can do,
Forever, with you.

They are standing at the altar together, looking directly at each other for the first time in the play.

JAMIE
Will you share your life with me
For the next ten lifetimes?
For a million summers

CATHERINE
Forever.
Forever, Jamie . . .

BOTH

'Til the world explodes,
'Til there's no one left
Who has ever known us apart!

JAMIE

There are so many dreams I need
to see
With you

I will never be complete—

CATHERINE

There are so many years
I need to be
With you . . .

CATHERINE

I will never be alive—

JAMIE

I will never change the world
Until I do.

CATHERINE

I do.

JAMIE

I do.

CATHERINE

I do.

BOTH

I do . . .

And they kiss, each holding on for as long

as possible, as if perhaps they knew they didn't have that long to go.

The orchestra plays a waltz, which they clumsily dance. He whispers something in her ear, she laughs and kisses him again. The waltz ends, and JAMIE *takes* CATHERINE*'s hand as she steps into the rowboat. As it starts to glide upstage,* JAMIE *stands and watches it go.* CATHERINE *looks across the boat as though* JAMIE *were in the other seat.*

CATHERINE

Is that one John Lennon?
That's the San Remo.
Isn't that the Museum?
Can we go see the dinosaurs?

The lights fade.

SCENE 9
A MIRACLE WOULD HAPPEN

Four months after the wedding. JAMIE *is at a bar talking to a friend.*

JAMIE

Everyone tells you that the minute you get married,
Every other woman in the world suddenly finds you attractive.
Well, that's not true.
It only affects the kind of women you always wanted to sleep
with,
But they wouldn't give you the time of day before,
And now they're banging down your door
And falling to their knees . . .
At least that's what it feels like because you
Can
Not
Touch
Them.
In fact, you can't even look at them--
Close your eyes, close your eyes, close your eyes.
Except you're sitting there,
Eating your corned beef sandwich,

And all of sudden this pair of breasts walks by and smiles at
you,
And you're like, "That's not fair!"

And in a perfect world,
A miracle would happen,
And every other girl would fly away,
And it'd be me and Cathy,
And nothing else would matter—
But it's fine, it's fine, it's fine,
I mean, I'm happy
And I'm fine, I'm fine, I'm fine—
It's not a problem, it's just a challenge—
It's a challenge to resist Temptation.

And I have to say that what exacerbates the problem
Is I'm at these parties, I'm the center of attention, I'm the
grand fromage,
And here she comes:
"Let's get a cup of coffee.
Will you look at my manuscript?"
And I'm showing her my left hand,
I'm gesticulating with my left hand,
And then *whoomp*! There's Cathy!
'Cause she knows—they always know—
And there's that really awkward moment
Where I try to show I wasn't encouraging this,
(Which of course I sort of was),
And I don't want to look whipped in front of this woman,
Which is dumb, I shouldn't care what she thinks
Since I can't fuck her anyway!

And in a perfect world,
A miracle would happen
And every girl would look like Mister Ed,
And it'd be me and Cathy,
And nothing else would matter.
But it's fine, it's fine, it's fine,
You know I love her
And it's fine, it's fine, it's fine—
It's what I wanted
And I'm fine, I'm fine, I'm fine!
It's not a problem, it's just a challenge—
It's a challenge to resist Temptation.

CATHERINE *sings "When You Come Home to Me," simply and perfectly—it is her final audition for the job in Ohio.*

CATHERINE

When you come home to me,
I'll wear a sweeter smile
And hope that, for a while, you'll stay.
When you come home to me,
Your hand will touch my face
And banish any trace of gray.
Soon, a love will rise anew
Even greater than the joy I felt
Just missing you,
And once again, I'll be
So proud to call you mine,

When finally you come home
To me.

She smiles when she is done—she knows she got the job.

JAMIE *is on the phone to* CATHERINE.

JAMIE

I'll be there soon, Cathy—
I'll finish up this chapter and be out the door.
I swear I'll be there soon, Cathy—
Don't give up on me yet.
I am so proud of you, baby—
You're doing what you never got to do before—
And I will be there, ripe and crawling,
If fuckin' Random House stops calling.
Don't lose faith—
Don't get down,
Don't despair:
I'll be there!

And in a perfect world,
A miracle would happen,
And that day would finally be here.
And it'd be me and you,
Riding it together,
And the things we do
Goin' like we planned.
We're gonna make it through,

"I didn't know you had to go so soon./I thought we had a little time . . ./Look, whatever, if you have to,/Then you have to, so whatever."

Sherie Rene Scott and Norbert Leo Butz in "See I'm Smiling."

“My heart’s been stolen!/My ego’s swollen!/I just keep rollin’ along!”

Norbert Leo Butz in “Moving Too Fast.”

"And then he smiles, / His eyes light up, and how can I complain? / Yes, he's insane, / But look what he can do."

Sherie Rene Scott in "A Part of That."

"Ev'ry cut and stitch was a perfect fit, / As if God Himself were controlling it! / And Schmuel cried, through a rush of tears, / 'Take me back! Take me back all forty-one years!'"

Norbert Leo Butz in "The Schmuel Song."

"There are so many lives I want to share with you—/I will never be complete until I do."

Sherie Rene Scott and Norbert Leo Butz in "The Next Ten Minutes."

"I want to be your wife./I want to bear your child./I want to die,/Knowing I/ had a long, full life in your arms."

Sherie Rene Scott and Norbert Leo Butz in "The Next Ten Minutes."

"Will you share your life with me/For the next ten lifetimes?/For a million summers/'Til the world explodes,/'Til there's no one left/Who has ever known us apart!"

Sherie Rene Scott and Norbert Leo Butz in "The Next Ten Minutes."

Sherie Rene Scott and Norbert Leo Butz.

And nothing else will matter—
We'll be fine, we're fine,
We're fine, we're fine,
We're fine, we're fine, we're fine . . .
I'll be there soon, Cathy
I swear I will . . .

The piano begins a very clunky rendition of "When You Come Home to Me" as the lights fade on JAMIE.

SCENE 10
CLIMBING UPHILL

CATHERINE is at an audition. She is incredibly nervous and cannot manage to get enough breath to project more than five feet in front of her or to quite get up to the pitch.

CATHERINE

WHEN YOU COME HOME TO ME,
I'LL WEAR A SWEETER SMILE
AND HOPE THAT, FOR A WHILE,
YOU'LL . . .

Okay, thank you. Thank you so much.

The lights change. She is having dinner with her father.

I'm climbin' uphill, Daddy.
Climbin' uphill.

I'm up ev'ry morning at six
And standing in line
With two hundred girls
Who are younger and thinner than me
Who have already been to the gym.

I'm waiting five hours in line,
And watching the girls
Just coming and going
In dresses that look *just like this,*
'Til my number is finally called.

When I walk in the room,
There's a table of men—
Always men, usually gay—
Who've been sitting, like I have,
And listening all day
To two hundred girls
Belting as high as they can!

I am a good person
I'm an attractive person.
I am a talented person
Grant me grace!

A bell tone. She steps forward and begins another audition. Instead of hearing the song, however, we hear what she's thinking.

When you come home . . .
I should have told them I was sick last week.
They're gonna think this is the way I sing.
Why is the pianist playing so loud?
Should I sing louder?
I'll sing louder.
Maybe I should stop and start over.
I'm going to stop and start over.
Why is the director staring at his crotch?
Why is that man staring at my résumé?
Don't stare at my résumé.
I made up half my résumé.
Look at me.
Stop looking at that, look at me.
No, not at my shoes.
Don't look at my shoes—
I hate these fucking shoes.
Why did I pick these shoes?
Why did I pick this song?
Why did I pick this career?
Why does this pianist hate me?
If I don't get a callback,
I can go to Crate and Barrel with Mom to buy a couch.
Not that I want to spend a day with Mom,
But Jamie needs his space to write,
Since I'm obviously such a horrible annoying distraction to him.
What's he gonna be like when we have kids?
And once again . . .
Why am I working so hard?
These are the people who cast Linda Blair in a musical.
Jesus Christ, I suck, I suck, I suck, I suck.

WHEN FIN'LLY YOU COME HOME
TO . . .

Okay. Thank you. Thank you so much.

JAMIE *is at his editor's office at Random House, on the phone to* CATHERINE.

JAMIE Cathy, what are you doing now? No, no—there's a bar across the street from Elise's office, and I want you to . . . I'm at Elise's office now. I came by to check something and . . . Well, just come down, I want to tell you in person, Cathy. Look, are you doing something right now? So just come . . . I'm with Elise because she is the editor of my book, Cathy, and I came here to talk to her about my book. Do we have to do this now? What I wanted to tell you is that there's a review, a very good review, in *The New Yorker* next week, and it's by John Updike, and I thought you might want to see that. Yes, I can bring it home with me, I just wanted to . . . No, I'm leaving now. I'll be there in a half hour. It's fine, I know, I know, it's fine. I love you, too. I'll be right home.

Lights fade on JAMIE.

CATHERINE
I will not be the girl stuck at home in the 'burbs
With the baby, the dog, and the garden of herbs.
I will not be the girl in the sensible shoes
Pushing burgers and beer nuts and missing the clues.
I will not be the girl who gets asked how it feels

To be trotting along at the genius's heels!
I will not be the girl who requires a man to get by,
And I . . .

Bell tone.

WHEN YOU COME HOME . . .

JAMIE *is doing a reading at a big bookstore. He sits on a stool behind a microphone. His relaxation and comfort stand in stark contrast to* CATHERINE*'s demeanor.*

JAMIE He touched the wall and decided he had had enough. He was exhausted, first of all, and he could feel it: his lungs were throbbing and heavy, and his left arm was stinging from the shoulder right down to his wrist. Besides that, seven laps in and the water was still freezing cold, and if he wanted to be honest about it, he felt foolish—a ghost-pale, graceless thing flapping about frantically, desperately trying to keep pace with the mermaid in the next lane. She was at least half a lap ahead of him, though he hadn't been able to keep track of her at all while he was swimming—every time he'd try to find her while he was catching a breath, she'd be completely out of range. But he could see her now, now that he was grabbing on to the side of the pool. He watched her back stretching, watched how she seemed to ride the water. Her arm came up over her ear and slid back under the surface soundlessly, effortlessly. Now she touched the opposite wall and was headed back towards him, and he watched as she changed her stroke, her head coming up and then submerging again in a burst of energy. He could see the shape of her face under her goggles, sense the curve of her breasts as she pushed up into the air. She didn't seem particularly familiar at that moment—he didn't recognize the fierceness in her brow, the tension in her biceps, the fury in the pumping of her calves. It had never occurred to him that three years on he would be learning new things about her. It hit him in that moment that there were so many things he would discover—how her stomach swelled when she was pregnant, for example, or how the skin around her eyes would wrinkle as the years passed. She touched the wall next to him and pushed off, but she must have sensed something and she looked behind her and saw him standing at the wall, one arm hanging off the side, his teeth chattering slightly. She slowed down and turned to face him, a quizzical smile crossing her lips. He smiled back at her as she pulled the goggles over her cap. Ah, he thought, there she is. I recognize her now. He would spend the rest of the day trying to determine what was driving her silence, her clenched jaw, her sharp turns away from him. You don't have to let me win, she was screaming, but he couldn't hear it at all.

He closes the book and looks up at his audience. CATHERINE*, meanwhile, is in the midst of vocalizing. She is trying to compensate for her previous mousiness with a hysterical stridency, which essentially forces* *her to scream every note at the loudest possible volume.*

CATHERINE

. . . AND BANISH ANY TRACE OF GRAY!
SOON A LOVE WILL RISE ANEW,
EVEN GREATER THAN THE JOY . . .

JAMIE *interrupts her and the lights change.*

SCENE 11
IF I DIDN'T BELIEVE IN YOU

A year before Scene 1. JAMIE *is in the middle of a fierce fight with* CATHERINE.

JAMIE Okay, stop. Cathy, stop. Listen to me. Can we please . . . could we have two minutes where you don't just contradict everything I say? Can we . . . Cathy! Please? Two minutes? Then it's your turn, you can say whatever you want.

There are people
And they are publishing my book
And there's a party
That they are throwing.
And while you've made it very clear that you're not going,
I will be going.
And that's done.

But what's it really about?
Is it really about a party, Cathy?
Can we please for a minute
Stop blaming and say what you feel?

Is it just that you're disappointed
To be touring again for the summer?
Did you think this would all be much easier
Than it's turned out to be?
Well, then talk to me, Cathy.
Talk to me.

If I didn't believe in you,
We'd never have gotten this far.
If I didn't believe in you
And all of the ten thousand women you are.
If I didn't think you could do
Anything you ever wanted to,
If I wasn't certain that you'd come through somehow,
The fact of the matter is, Cathy,
I wouldn't be standing here now.

If I didn't believe in you,
We wouldn't be having this fight.
If I didn't believe in you,
I'd walk out the door and say, "Cathy, you're right."
But I never could let that go
Knowing the things about you I know—
Things, when I met you four years ago, I knew.
It never took much convincing
To make me believe in you.

Don't we get to be happy, Cathy?
At some point down the line,
Don't we get to relax
Without some new tsuris

To push me yet further from you?
If I'm cheering on your side, Cathy,
Why can't you support mine?
Why do I have to feel
I committed some felony
Doing what I always swore I would do?

I don't want you to hurt,
I don't want you to sink,
But you know what I think?
I think you'll be fine!
Just hang on and you'll see—
But don't make me wait 'til you do
To be happy with you—
Will you listen to me?
No one can give you courage
No one can thicken your skin.
I will not fail so you can be comfortable, Cathy.
I will not lose because you can't win.

If I didn't believe in you,
Then here's where the travelogue ends.
If I didn't believe in you,
I couldn't have stood before all of our friends
And said, "This is the life I choose—
This is the thing I can't bear to lose.
Trip us or trap us, but we refuse to fall."
That's what I thought we agreed on, Cathy.
If I hadn't believed in you,
I wouldn't have loved you at all.

Now why don't you put on your dress and we'll go, okay?
Cathy? Can we do that, please? Please?

But she's not going anywhere, and he has probably known that all along.

Blackout.

SCENE 12
I CAN DO BETTER THAN THAT

Five months after Scene 2. CATHERINE, *driving* JAMIE *to meet her parents. She rambles and babbles happily throughout.*

CATHERINE

My best friend had a little situation at the end of our senior year,
And like a shot, she and Mitchell got married that summer.
Carolann getting bigger ev'ry minute, thinking, "What am I doing here?"
While Mitchell's out ev'ry night, being a heavy-metal drummer.
They got a little cute house on a little cute street with a crucifix on the door,
Mitchell got a job at a record store in the mall.
Just the typical facts of a typical life in a town on the Eastern Shore—
I thought about what I wanted,
It wasn't like that at all.

Made Carolann a cute baby sweater,
Thinking, "I can do better than that."

I wasn't paying attention, what exit was that?
All right, so we'll be there soon. Are you hungry? Sick of me yet?
Anyway.

In a year or so, I moved to the city, thinking, "What have I got to lose?"
Got a room, got a cat, and got twenty pounds thinner.
Met a guy in a class I was taking with some very well-placed tattoos—
He wouldn't leave me alone 'less I went with him to dinner.
And I guess he was cute, and I guess he was sweet, and I guess he was good in bed—
I gave up my life for the better part of a year.
So I'm starting to feel like this maybe might work, and the second it entered my head,
He needed to take some time off,
Focus on his "career"—
He blew me off with a heartfelt letter—
I thought, "I can do better than that."

You don't have to get a haircut,
You don't have to change your shoes,
You don't have to like Duran Duran,
Just love me.

You don't have to put the seat down,
You don't have to watch the news,
You don't have to learn to tango,

You don't have to eat prosciutto,
You don't have to change a thing,
Just stay with me.

I want you and you and nothing but you,
Miles and piles of you—
Finally I'll have something worthwhile
To think of each morning—

You and you and nothing but you,
No substitution will do,
Nothing but fresh, undiluted, and pure,
Top of the line,
And totally mine!

I don't need any lifetime commitments, I don't need to get hitched tonight,
I don't want you to throw up all your walls and defenses.
I don't mean to put on any pressure, but I know when a thing is right—
And I spend every day reconfiguring my senses.
When we get to my house, take a look at that town, take a look at how far I've gone—
I will never go back, never look back anymore.
And it feels like my life led right to your side and will keep me there from now on.
Think about what you wanted,
Think about what could be,
Think about how I love you—
Say you'll move in with me.
Think of what's great about me and you,
Think of the bullshit we've both been through,

Think of what's past, because we can do
Better!
We can do better!
We can do better than that!
We can do better than that!

Blackout.

SCENE 13
NOBODY NEEDS TO KNOW

Lights rise on JAMIE *in bed, his shirt off. He opens his eyes, looks at the clock and then at the woman in bed beside him.*

JAMIE

Hey, kid—good morning—
You look like an angel.
I don't remember when we fell asleep.
We should get up, kid—
Cathy is waiting . . .

Look at us, lying here,
Dreaming, pretending.
I made a promise and I took a vow.
I wrote a story,
And we changed the ending—
Cathy, just look at me now!

Hold on, facts are facts—
Just relax, lay low.

All right, the panic recedes:
Nobody needs to know.

Put on my armor—
I'm off to Ohio.
Back into battle 'til I don't know when.
Swearing to her that I
Never was with you,
And praying I'll hold you again.

Hold on, clip these wings—
Things get out of hand.
All right, it's over, it's done—
No one will understand.
No one will understand . . .

We build a tree house,
I keep it from shaking—
Little more glue ev'ry time that it breaks.
Perfectly balanced,
And then I start making
Conscious, deliberate mistakes.

All that I ask for
Is one little corner—
One private room at the back of my heart.
Tell her I found one,
She sends out battalions
To claim it and blow it apart.

I grip and she grips,
And faster we're sliding.

Sliding and spilling, and what can I do?
Come back to bed, kid—
Take me inside you—
I promise I won't lie to you.

Hold on, don't cry yet—
I won't let you go.
All right—the panic recedes;
All right—everyone bleeds;
All right—I get what I need,
And nobody needs
To know.
Nobody needs to know . . .

And since I have to be in love with someone,
Since I need to be in love with someone,
Maybe I could be in love with someone
Like you . . .

The light fades on the bed, and rises on the steps in front of CATHERINE*'s apartment.*

SCENE 14

GOODBYE UNTIL TOMORROW/ I COULD NEVER RESCUE YOU

On CATHERINE*'s front steps at the end of the first date.* JAMIE *has just kissed* CATHERINE.

CATHERINE

Don't kiss me goodbye again.
Leave this night clean and quiet.
You want the last word,
You want me to laugh,
But leave it for now.

All you can say,
All you can feel
Was wrapped up inside that one perfect kiss.
Leave it at that:
I'll watch you turn the corner and go . . .

And goodbye until tomorrow.
Goodbye until the next time you call,
And I will be waiting.

I will be waiting.
Goodbye until tomorrow.
Goodbye 'til I recall how to breathe,
And I have been waiting,
I have been waiting for you.

She watches him go.

I stand on a precipice.
I struggle to keep my balance.
I open myself,
I open myself one stitch at a time.

Finally yes!
Finally now!
Finally something takes me away.
Finally free!
Finally he can cut through these strings,
And open my wings!

So goodbye until tomorrow!
Goodbye until my feet touch the floor,
And I will be waiting,
I will be waiting!
Goodbye until tomorrow!
Goodbye until the rest of my life
And I have been waiting,

I have been waiting for you!
Waiting for you,
Waiting for you!

JAMIE appears at the table. He is writing a note on a yellow pad on the table—his wedding ring is on the table next to it, where it was at the beginning of the show.

JAMIE

I called Elise to help me pack my bags.
I went downtown and closed the bank account.
It's not about another shrink,
It's not about another compromise.
I'm not the only one who's hurting here.
I don't know what the hell is left to do.
You never saw how far the crack had opened.
You never knew I had run out of rope and

I could never rescue you.
All you ever wanted,
But I could never rescue you,
No matter how I tried.
All I could do was love you hard
And let you go.

He puts down the pen, stands, and looks around the empty apartment.

No matter how I tried,
All I could do was love you.

God, I loved you so.
So we could fight,
Or we could wait,
Or I could go . . .

CATHERINE

Goodbye until tomorrow!
Goodbye until I crawl to your door,
And I will be waiting,
I will be waiting!

JAMIE

You never noticed how
The wind had changed.

CATHERINE

Goodbye until tomorrow!

JAMIE

I didn't see a way we
both could win.

CATHERINE

Goodbye until I'm done thanking
God,
For I have been waiting!
I have been waiting for you!

JAMIE

Goodbye, Cathy.

CATHERINE

I have been waiting!
I have been waiting for you!

JAMIE

Goodbye . . .

CATHERINE

I will keep waiting—
I will be waiting for you!

He picks up his briefcase and knapsack and slowly begins to cross the stage, passing her front steps.

Just close the gate;
I'll stand and wait.

She is looking off, where she watched him go—he is looking up at her on her steps.

Jamie . . .

BOTH

Goodbye.

Blackout.

End of play.